ANCESTRAL TIES

A JOURNEY THROUGH INDIA'S GOTRA SYSTEM

DR. JAGADEESH PILLAI

Made with ❤ on the Notion Press Platform
www.notionpress.com

|| "Dedicated to all who seek to understand and appreciate Indian culture and tradition." ||

‍‌ॐ

Contents

Contents

PRAYER

**"Om Bhadram Karnebhih Shrunuyaama
DevaahBhadram Pashyemaakshabhiryajatraah
SthirairangaistushtuvaamsastanoobhihVyashema
Devahitam YadaayuhSwasti Na Indro
VridhashravaahSwasti Nah Pooshaa
VishwavedaahSwasti Nastaarkshyo ArishtanemihSwasti
No Brihaspatir DadhaatuOm Shantih, Shantih, Shantih"**

The literal meaning of this mantra is: OM. O Gods! Let us
hear auspicious words from our ears. O reverent Gods! Let
us behold propitious visions from our eyes, let our organs
and body be stable, healthy, and strong. Let us do that
which is pleasing to the gods in the life span allotted to us.
May Indra, inscribed in the scriptures, bring us fortune!
May Pushan, the knower of the world, grant us prosperity!
May Trakshya, who vanquishes enemies, bestow us with
blessings! May Brihaspati bring us success!
OM Peace, Peace, Peace.

About The Author

Dr. Jagadeesh Pillai is a renowned Guinness World Record holder, writer, and researcher hailing from Varanasi, also known as the abode of Lord Shiva. With a Ph.D. in Vedic Science and a range of creative ideas and achievements, he is a true polymath. He is the author of more than 100 books including Research Publications. Although his roots can be traced back to Kerala, the people of Varanasi hold him in high regard and affectionately consider him one of their own.

Dr. Pillai has achieved four Guinness World Records in the following subjects:

"Script to Screen" - In this record, Dr. Pillai produced and directed an animation film within the shortest time possible, breaking the previous record set by Canadians. He has also received numerous national and international awards and recognitions for this achievement.

Longest Line of Postcards - For this record, Dr. Pillai created a line of 16,300 postcards on the occasion of the 163rd anniversary of Indian Postal Day. The event also included a questionnaire about the Indian flag.

Largest Poster Awareness Campaign - Dr. Pillai designed an awareness campaign on the subject of "Beti Bachao - Beti Padhao" (Save the Girl Child - Educate the Girl Child) to achieve this record.

Largest Envelope - In tribute to the Indian Prime Minister's

"Make in India" initiative, Dr. Pillai created a 4000 square meter envelope using waste paper to achieve this record.

Attempted - **70000 Candles on a 210 kg Cake** - To celebrate the 70th Indian Independence Day, Dr. Pillai attempted to light 70,000 candles on a 210 kg cake, which was recorded in World Records India.

Attempted - **Documentary on Dhamek Stupa of Sarnath in 17 Languages** - Dr. Pillai attempted to create a documentary on the Dhamek Stupa of Sarnath, dubbing it in 17 different languages. The result of this attempt is currently awaiting confirmation from the Guinness World Records.

Dr. Pillai is skilled in teaching the Bhagavad Gita, a Hindu scripture, and is popular among young people. He has helped many young people improve their lives through his motivational teachings.

In addition to teaching, he has composed and sung numerous Sanskrit Bhajans and patriotic songs.

He has also written and directed several short films and documentaries for awareness campaigns, and has volunteered with the police in both UP and Kerala to spread awareness about various issues through videos and photography.

Incredibly, he has produced and directed over 100 documentaries about the city of Varanasi, all on his own.

He has also helped and guided more than 25 boys and girls to achieve world records through creative and innovative methods. He is a multifaceted person who uses his intellect and the blessings given to him by God to excel in various areas. He is both a teacher and a student, always learning and teaching, and is able to master any subject he comes across.

He is a selfless social activist and motivational speaker who has overcome struggles and failures to become a successful and enthusiastic individual with a rich life experience.

In addition to his work with the Bhagavad Gita, he is also an efficient Tarot card reader, Astro-Vastu consultant, and a talented singer and composer. He has sung the entire Ram Charita Manas and Bhagavad Gita in his own compositions, and has sung the phrase "Lokah Samastha Sukhino Bhavantu" in 50 different languages. He is currently working on a detailed and scientific study of Vedas, Upanishads, Puranas, and the Bhagavad Gita. He has also composed and sung the Hanuman Chalisa and Gayatri Mantra in 108 and 1008 different compositions, respectively.

Awards - Four Times Guinness World Records, Winner of Mahatma Gandhi Vishwa Shanti Puraskar, Mahatma Gandhi Global Peace Ambassador, Kashi Ratna Award, Dr. APJ Abdul Kalam Motivational Person of the Year 2017, Mother Teresa Award, Indira Gandhi Priyadarshini Award, Bharat Vikas Ratna Award, Udyog Ratna Award, Vigyan Prasar Award, Poorvanchal Ratn Samman.

Preface

The Gotra system, which traces lineage from a common male ancestor, is an important aspect of social identity in many parts of India. This book aims to provide an in-depth understanding of the Gotra system in India, including its origins, significance, and impact on society and culture.

In this book, we explore the Gotra system in various regions of India, including North India, South India, West India, and East India. We also examine the role of Gotras in Indian marriage customs and its relationship with the caste system. The book also delves into the issues of Gotra-based discrimination and the contemporary perspective on Gotra preservation and revival.

We hope that this book will serve as a valuable resource for those interested in understanding the Gotra system and its impact on Indian society and culture. It will also provide insights for individuals and communities to strike a balance between preserving their Gotra heritage and promoting inclusivity and equality in society.

This book is a result of extensive research and analysis, and we hope that it will be informative and engaging for readers. We believe that it will be a useful resource for researchers, students, and anyone interested in understanding the complexities of the Gotra system and its impact on Indian society and culture.

Disclaimer

The information provided in this book is intended to be a general overview of the Gotra system prevalent in India. However, it is important to note that there may be variations in Gotra names and their application to different castes. The information provided in this book should not be considered as a definitive or exhaustive study of Gotras. To know about a particular Gotra and its details, we recommend consulting a family priest or any elder in the house. The author and publisher of this book are not responsible for any inaccuracies or errors in the information provided.

I

Introduction to the Gotra System in India

The Gotra system is an ancient system of tracing one's lineage and ancestry in India. The term "Gotra" is derived from the Sanskrit word "Gōtra" which means "cow pen" or "herd of cows". In the traditional Indian society, Gotras were used to trace the lineage of a person and were an important aspect of social identity.

In Hinduism, Gotras are used to trace the lineage of a person from a common male ancestor. The Gotra system is patrilineal, meaning that a person's Gotra is passed down from their father. Each Gotra is associated with a specific Rishi or sage, who is considered to be the founder of the Gotra.

Gotras are traditionally divided into eight major Gotras and each Gotra is further divided into sub-Gotras or branches. The eight major Gotras are: Bharadwaja, Kashyapa, Vashishtha, Gautama, Atri, Kutsa, Vasistha, and Jamadagni.

Gotras are not limited to Hindus, and they are also found in other Indian religions such as Jainism and Buddhism. In Jainism and Buddhism, Gotras are used to trace the lineage of a person from a common male ancestor and are passed down from father to son.

The Gotra system plays an important role in the traditional Indian society. It is used to determine the suitability of a marriage partner, as people from the same Gotra are considered to be of the same lineage and are not allowed to marry. This practice is known as Gotra exogamy.

Gotra exogamy is a custom that is still prevalent in many parts of India, and it is considered to be an important aspect of social identity. However, with the changing times, this custom is being challenged, and many people are breaking the tradition and marrying within their Gotras.

Gotra exogamy is not followed in all regions of India, and there are many communities and tribes that follow Gotra endogamy, where people are allowed to marry within their Gotras.

In addition to marriage customs, Gotras also play a role in social and political events. In many parts of India, Gotra-based discrimination is a serious issue and it is important to address it in order to create a more inclusive society.

The Gotra system is an ancient system of tracing one's

lineage and ancestry in India. It is an important aspect of social identity and is traditionally used to determine the suitability of a marriage partner. Gotras are used not only in Hinduism but also in Jainism and Buddhism. Gotra exogamy is a custom that is still prevalent in many parts of India but it is slowly being challenged and many people are breaking the tradition. Gotra system play a role in social and political events and it's important to address the Gotra-based discrimination to make a more inclusive society.

"Traditions are the guideposts driven deep in
our subconscious minds. The most powerful
ones are those we can't even describe, aren't
even aware of."

- Ellen Goodman

II

The Origin and Evolution of Gotras in Hinduism

The Gotra system in Hinduism is an ancient system of tracing one's lineage and ancestry. It is believed to have originated in Vedic times, and the earliest mention of Gotras can be found in the Vedas, the ancient Hindu texts. The Gotras were used to trace the lineage of a person from a common male ancestor, and were an important aspect of social identity.

The origin of Gotras can be traced back to the Rishis or sages of ancient India. The Rishis were considered to be the founders of Gotras, and each Gotra was named after a specific Rishi. The Rishis were believed to be the spiritual leaders and teachers of ancient India, and they were considered to be the custodians of knowledge and wisdom. They were also believed to be the creators of the Vedic hymns and mantras.

The Rishis were divided into different groups, known as Shakhas, and each Shakha had a specific Gotra. The Gotras were passed down from father to son, and the Rishi who was the founder of the Gotra was considered to be the spiritual ancestor of the people who belonged to that Gotra.

Over time, the Gotra system evolved and became more complex. The eight major Gotras, Bharadwaja, Kashyapa, Vashishtha, Gautama, Atri, Kutsa, Vasistha and Jamadagni, were further divided into sub-Gotras or branches. Each sub-Gotra had its own specific rituals and customs.

With the passage of time, the Gotra system became an important aspect of social identity and was used to determine the suitability of a marriage partner. The practice of Gotra exogamy, where people from the same Gotra were not allowed to marry, was widely followed in ancient India.

In the present day, Gotras continue to be an important aspect of social identity in Hinduism. However, the custom of Gotra exogamy is being challenged and many people are breaking the tradition and marrying within their Gotras. Also, the Gotra system is not limited to Hinduism and it is also found in other Indian religions such as Jainism and Buddhism.

The Gotra system in Hinduism is an ancient system of tracing one's lineage and ancestry. It originated in Vedic times and was believed to have been established by the Rishis, the sages of ancient India. The Gotra system evolved over time, and it became an important aspect of social identity and was used to determine the suitability of a marriage partner, but this custom of Gotra exogamy is being challenged in present day. Gotra system is not limited to Hinduism but also found in other Indian religions such as Jainism and Buddhism.

"The roots of all religions are the same, and the traditions are different."

- Jiddu Krishnamurti

III

Gotras in North India: A Study of Punjab, Haryana and Uttar Pradesh

The Gotra system is an important aspect of social identity in North India, particularly in the states of Punjab, Haryana, and Uttar Pradesh. The Gotra system in these states is closely linked to the caste system and is used to trace the lineage of a person from a common male ancestor.

In Punjab, Haryana, and Uttar Pradesh, the Gotra system is prevalent among the Hindu, Sikh and Jat communities. The Jat community, in particular, is known to be very conscious of their Gotras, and they use Gotras to determine the suitability of a marriage partner. The practice of Gotra exogamy is widely followed in these states, and people from the same Gotra are not allowed to marry.

In Punjab and Haryana, the Gotra system is closely linked to the caste system and is used to determine the social status of a person. A person's Gotra is considered to be an indicator of their caste and social status. The Gotra system is also used to determine the economic status of a person, as people from higher castes and Gotras are considered to be more affluent.

In Uttar Pradesh, the Gotra system is closely linked to the caste system and is used to determine the social status of a person. The Gotra system is also used to determine the suitability of a marriage partner, and the practice of Gotra exogamy is widely followed in this state.

The Gotra system in North India is also closely linked to the concept of 'Khandaan' or family, and the Gotra is considered to be an important aspect of one's identity. The Gotra system is also closely linked to the concept of 'Kuldevta' or family deity, and people from the same Gotra are expected to worship the same deity.

The Gotra system is an important aspect of social identity in North India, particularly in the states of Punjab, Haryana, and Uttar Pradesh. The Gotra system is closely linked to the caste system and is used to trace the lineage of a person from a common male ancestor. The practice of Gotra exogamy is widely followed in these states, and the Gotra system is also closely linked to the concept of 'Khandaan' or family and 'Kuldevta' or family deity. The Gotra system is prevalent among the Hindu, Sikh and Jat communities.

"Tradition is not the worship of ashes, but the preservation of fire."

- Gustav Mahler

IV

Gotras in South India: A Study of Tamil Nadu and Andhra Pradesh

The Gotra system is an important aspect of social identity in South India, particularly in the states of Tamil Nadu and Andhra Pradesh. The Gotra system in these states is closely linked to the caste system and is used to trace the lineage of a person from a common male ancestor.

In Tamil Nadu and Andhra Pradesh, the Gotra system is prevalent among the Brahmin, Vellala and Thevar communities. The Gotra system is used to determine the suitability of a marriage partner, and the practice of Gotra exogamy is widely followed in these states. People from the same Gotra are not allowed to marry.

In Tamil Nadu, the Gotra system is closely linked to the caste system, and a person's Gotra is considered to be an indicator of their caste and social status. The Gotra system is also used to determine the economic status of a person, as people from higher castes and Gotras are considered to be more affluent.

In Andhra Pradesh, the Gotra system is used to determine the social status of a person. The Gotra system is also used to determine the suitability of a marriage partner, and the practice of Gotra exogamy is widely followed in this state.

The Gotra system in South India is also closely linked to the concept of 'Kula' or family, and the Gotra is considered to be an important aspect of one's identity. The Gotra system is also closely linked to the concept of 'Kuladevata' or family deity, and people from the same Gotra are expected to worship the same deity.

The Gotra system is an important aspect of social identity in South India, particularly in the states of Tamil Nadu and Andhra Pradesh. The Gotra system is closely linked to the caste system and is used to trace the lineage of a person from a common male ancestor. The practice of Gotra exogamy is widely followed in these states, and the Gotra system is also closely linked to the concept of 'Kula' or family and 'Kuladevata' or family deity. The Gotra system is prevalent among the Brahmin, Vellala and Thevar communities.

"Culture is the sum of all the forms of art, of love, and of thought, which, in the course of centuries, have enabled man to be less enslaved."

- André Malraux

ॐ

V
Gotras in West India: A Study of Maharashtra and Gujarat

The Gotra system is an important aspect of social identity in West India, particularly in the states of Maharashtra and Gujarat. The Gotra system in these states is closely linked to the caste system and is used to trace the lineage of a person from a common male ancestor.

In Maharashtra and Gujarat, the Gotra system is prevalent among the Brahmin, Maratha, and Patidar communities. The Gotra system is used to determine the suitability of a marriage partner, and the practice of Gotra exogamy is widely followed in these states. People from the same Gotra are not allowed to marry.

In Maharashtra, the Gotra system is closely linked to the caste system, and a person's Gotra is considered to be an indicator of their caste and social status. The Gotra system is also used to determine the economic status of a person, as people from higher castes and Gotras are considered to be more affluent.

In Gujarat, the Gotra system is used to determine the social status of a person. The Gotra system is also used to determine the suitability of a marriage partner, and the practice of Gotra exogamy is widely followed in this state.

The Gotra system in West India is also closely linked to the concept of 'Kul' or family, and the Gotra is considered to be an important aspect of one's identity. The Gotra system is also closely linked to the concept of 'Kuldevta' or family deity, and people from the same Gotra are expected to worship the same deity.

The Gotra system is an important aspect of social identity in West India, particularly in the states of Maharashtra and Gujarat. The Gotra system is closely linked to the caste system and is used to trace the lineage of a person from a common male ancestor. The practice of Gotra exogamy is widely followed in these states, and the Gotra system is also closely linked to the concept of 'Kul' or family and 'Kuldevta' or family deity. The Gotra system is prevalent among the Brahmin, Maratha, and Patidar communities.

"Tradition is the illusion of permanence."

- Woody Allen

ॐ

VI

Gotras in East India: A Study of Odisha and West Bengal

The Gotra system is an important aspect of social identity in East India, particularly in the states of Odisha and West Bengal. The Gotra system in these states is closely linked to the caste system and is used to trace the lineage of a person from a common male ancestor.

In Odisha and West Bengal, the Gotra system is prevalent among the Kshatriya and Brahmin communities. The Gotra system is used to determine the suitability of a marriage partner, and the practice of Gotra exogamy is widely followed in these states. People from the same Gotra are not allowed to marry.

In Odisha, the Gotra system is closely linked to the caste system, and a person's Gotra is considered to be an indicator of their caste and social status. The Gotra system is also used to determine the economic status of a person, as people from higher castes and Gotras are considered to be more affluent.

In West Bengal, the Gotra system is used to determine the social status of a person. The Gotra system is also used to determine the suitability of a marriage partner, and the practice of Gotra exogamy is widely followed in this state.

The Gotra system in East India is also closely linked to the concept of 'Kula' or family, and the Gotra is considered to be an important aspect of one's identity. The Gotra system is also closely linked to the concept of 'Kuladevata' or family deity, and people from the same Gotra are expected to worship the same deity.

The Gotra system is an important aspect of social identity in East India, particularly in the states of Odisha and West Bengal. The Gotra system is closely linked to the caste system and is used to trace the lineage of a person from a common male ancestor. The practice of Gotra exogamy is widely followed in these states, and the Gotra system is also closely linked to the concept of 'Kula' or family and 'Kuladevata' or family deity. The Gotra system is prevalent among the Kshatriya and Brahmin communities in these states. However, it's worth noting that the prevalence and significance of Gotra system may vary among different communities and regions within these states.

"Rituals are important. Nowadays it's hip not
to be married. I'm not interested in being hip."

- John Lennon

VII

The Role of Gotras in Indian Marriage Customs

The Gotra system plays a significant role in Indian marriage customs, particularly in Hindu and Jain communities. The Gotra system is used to trace the lineage of a person from a common male ancestor and is an important aspect of social identity.

One of the main roles of Gotras in Indian marriage customs is determining the suitability of a marriage partner. The practice of Gotra exogamy is widely followed in many parts of India, which means that people from the same Gotra are not allowed to marry. This practice is based on the belief that people from the same Gotra are considered to be of the same lineage and are considered to be blood relatives.

Gotra exogamy is considered to be an important aspect of

social identity and is still prevalent in many parts of India. However, with the changing times, this custom is being challenged, and many people are breaking the tradition and marrying within their Gotras.

Another important aspect of Gotras in Indian marriage customs is the concept of 'Kuldevta' or family deity. People from the same Gotra are expected to worship the same deity, and this is considered to be an important aspect of the Gotra system.

In addition to marriage customs, Gotras also play a role in social and political events. In many parts of India, Gotra-based discrimination is a serious issue, and it is important to address it in order to create a more inclusive society.

The Gotra system plays a significant role in Indian marriage customs, particularly in Hindu and Jain communities. The Gotra system is used to determine the suitability of a marriage partner, and the practice of Gotra exogamy is widely followed in many parts of India. The Gotra system is also closely linked to the concept of 'Kuldevta' or family deity, and people from the same Gotra are expected to worship the same deity. While the Gotra system is an important aspect of social identity, it is important to recognize that the practice of Gotra exogamy can perpetuate discrimination and exclusivity, and efforts should be made to promote inclusivity and equality in regards to marriage and other social and political events.

"Tradition is the democracy of the dead."

- G.K. Chesterton

VIII

The Role of Gotras in Indian Marriage Customs

The Gotra system plays a significant role in Indian marriage customs, particularly in Hindu and Jain communities. The Gotra system is used to trace the lineage of a person from a common male ancestor and is an important aspect of social identity.

One of the main roles of Gotras in Indian marriage customs is determining the suitability of a marriage partner. The practice of Gotra exogamy is widely followed in many parts of India, which means that people from the same Gotra are not allowed to marry. This practice is based on the belief that people from the same Gotra are considered to be of the same lineage and are considered to be blood relatives.

Gotra exogamy is considered to be an important aspect of

social identity and is still prevalent in many parts of India. However, with the changing times, this custom is being challenged, and many people are breaking the tradition and marrying within their Gotras.

Another important aspect of Gotras in Indian marriage customs is the concept of 'Kuldevta' or family deity. People from the same Gotra are expected to worship the same deity, and this is considered to be an important aspect of the Gotra system.

In addition to marriage customs, Gotras also play a role in social and political events. In many parts of India, Gotra-based discrimination is a serious issue, and it is important to address it in order to create a more inclusive society.

The Gotra system plays a significant role in Indian marriage customs, particularly in Hindu and Jain communities. The Gotra system is used to determine the suitability of a marriage partner, and the practice of Gotra exogamy is widely followed in many parts of India. The Gotra system is also closely linked to the concept of 'Kuldevta' or family deity, and people from the same Gotra are expected to worship the same deity. While the Gotra system is an important aspect of social identity, it is important to recognize that the practice of Gotra exogamy can perpetuate discrimination and exclusivity, and efforts should be made to promote inclusivity and equality in regards to marriage and other social and political events.

"Tradition is a guide and not a jailer."

- W. Somerset Maugham

IX

The Gotra System in Jainism and Buddhism

The Gotra system, which traces lineage from a common male ancestor, is an important aspect of social identity in many parts of India, including in Jainism and Buddhism.

In Jainism, the Gotra system is used to determine the suitability of a marriage partner, and the practice of Gotra exogamy is widely followed. People from the same Gotra are not allowed to marry as they are considered to be of the same lineage and are considered to be blood relatives. The Gotra system is also closely linked to the concept of 'Kuldevta' or family deity, and people from the same Gotra are expected to worship the same deity.

In Buddhism, the Gotra system is not as prominent as it is in Hinduism and Jainism. However, in certain regions of

India, particularly in the state of Maharashtra, the Gotra system is still used to determine the suitability of a marriage partner among the Buddhist community.

It's worth noting that the Gotra system is not an integral part of the teachings of Jainism and Buddhism, and its importance and practice may vary among different regions and communities.

The Gotra system, which traces lineage from a common male ancestor, is an important aspect of social identity in Jainism and Buddhism. In Jainism, the Gotra system is used to determine the suitability of a marriage partner, and the practice of Gotra exogamy is widely followed. In Buddhism, the Gotra system is not as prominent as it is in Hinduism and Jainism but is still used in certain regions of India.

"Traditions are the guideposts driven deep in our subconscious minds. The most powerful ones are those we can't even describe, aren't even aware of."

- Ellen Goodman

X

The Impact of Gotras on Indian Society and Culture

The Gotra system, which traces lineage from a common male ancestor, has had a significant impact on Indian society and culture.

One of the main impacts of Gotras on Indian society is the practice of Gotra exogamy, which is widely followed in many parts of India. This practice is based on the belief that people from the same Gotra are considered to be of the same lineage and are considered to be blood relatives. This has led to the creation of a social hierarchy based on Gotras, where people from higher Gotras are considered to be of a higher social status.

Gotras also play a significant role in determining the suitability of a marriage partner. The practice of Gotra exogamy is widely followed in many parts of India, and people from the same Gotra are not allowed to marry. This has led to the preservation of certain Gotras and the disappearance of others.

The Gotra system is also closely linked to the concept of 'Kuldevta' or family deity, and people from the same Gotra are expected to worship the same deity. This has led to the preservation of certain deities and the disappearance of others.

In addition to its impact on society and culture, Gotras have also had an impact on politics. In many parts of India, Gotra-based discrimination is a serious issue, and it is important to address it in order to create a more inclusive society.

The Gotra system has had a significant impact on Indian society and culture. It has led to the creation of a social hierarchy based on Gotras, the preservation of certain Gotras, the practice of Gotra exogamy, the preservation of certain deities, and has also contributed to issues of discrimination in politics. While the Gotra system is an important aspect of social identity in India, it is important to recognize that its rigid adherence to certain customs and practices can perpetuate discrimination and exclusivity. It's important to strive for inclusivity and equality in society and culture, rather than getting bogged down by the Gotra system.

"India is the mother of all civilizations. India is the fountain of the world's cultures. India is the seed-ground of the world's religions."

- Mahatma Gandhi

౫

XI

Gotra Exogamy and Endogamy: A Comparative Study

The Gotra system, which traces lineage from a common male ancestor, is an important aspect of social identity in many parts of India. One of the main practices associated with the Gotra system is Gotra exogamy, which is the practice of not marrying within one's own Gotra. This is commonly contrasted with Gotra endogamy, which is the practice of marrying within one's own Gotra. This chapter aims to compare and contrast these two practices in terms of their origins, significance, and effects on society.

Gotra exogamy is believed to have originated from the belief that people from the same Gotra are considered to be of the same lineage and are considered to be blood relatives. This practice is widely followed in many parts of India and is considered to be an important aspect of social identity. It is used to determine the suitability of a marriage partner and to preserve certain Gotras.

Gotra endogamy, on the other hand, is a relatively modern practice that is becoming more common in certain regions of India. It is the practice of marrying within one's own Gotra, and it is often seen as a rejection of the traditional practice of Gotra exogamy. This practice is often associated with progressive and liberal thinking and a rejection of outdated social norms.

In terms of effects on society, Gotra exogamy has led to the creation of a social hierarchy based on Gotras, the preservation of certain Gotras, and the practice of Gotra exogamy. Gotra endogamy, on the other hand, challenges traditional social norms and promotes inclusivity and equality.

Gotra exogamy and Gotra endogamy are two practices associated with the Gotra system that have distinct origins and significance. Gotra exogamy is the traditional practice of not marrying within one's own Gotra, while Gotra endogamy is a relatively modern practice of marrying within one's own Gotra. Both practices have an effect on society, with Gotra exogamy leading to the creation of a social hierarchy and preservation of certain Gotras and Gotra endogamy challenging traditional norms and promoting inclusivity and equality. It's important to recognize that these practices are not mutually exclusive and that individuals and communities may adopt a combination of both. Ultimately, the choice of marriage partner should be based on mutual consent and compatibility rather than solely on Gotra.

"*India is the cradle of the human race, the birthplace of human speech, the mother of history, the grandmother of legend, and the great-grandmother of tradition.*"

- Mark Twain

ॐ

XII

The Relationship between Gotras and Castes

The Gotra system, which traces lineage from a common male ancestor, and the caste system, which is a social hierarchy based on birth, are both important aspects of social identity in many parts of India. However, the relationship between Gotras and castes is complex and varies depending on the region and community.

In some parts of India, Gotras are closely linked to the caste system, and a person's Gotra is considered to be an indicator of their caste and social status. People from higher castes and Gotras are considered to be more affluent and have more social and economic power. In these areas, the practice of Gotra exogamy is also closely linked to the practice of endogamy within castes, as people from different castes and Gotras are not allowed to marry.

In other parts of India, Gotras are not as closely linked to the caste system, and people from different castes can belong to the same Gotra. In these areas, the practice of Gotra exogamy is more focused on preserving the Gotra rather than maintaining the caste hierarchy.

It's worth noting that the relationship between Gotras and castes is not fixed and may change over time and vary within different regions and communities. The caste system has been abolished by the Indian government in 1950 through a legislation, however it's still prevalent in many parts of the country.

The relationship between Gotras and castes is complex and varies depending on the region and community. In some parts of India, Gotras are closely linked to the caste system and in others, they are not. The practice of Gotra exogamy may also be closely linked to the practice of endogamy within castes in some areas, while in others it is focused on preserving the Gotra. It's important to recognize that the relationship between Gotras and castes may change over time and vary within different regions and communities.

"India is a land of ancient culture and
wisdom, and these are qualities that cannot
be easily bought or sold."

- Dalai Lama

XIII

Gotra-based Discrimination in India: A Critical Analysis"

The Gotra system, which traces lineage from a common male ancestor, is an important aspect of social identity in many parts of India. However, the rigid adherence to Gotra-based customs and practices can perpetuate discrimination and exclusivity in society. This chapter aims to critically analyze the issue of Gotra-based discrimination in India.

Gotra-based discrimination can take various forms, such as social exclusion, economic discrimination, and even violence. One of the main reasons for Gotra-based discrimination is the practice of Gotra exogamy, which is the practice of not marrying within one's own Gotra. This practice can lead to the marginalization of certain Gotras and the exclusion of individuals from certain social and economic opportunities.

Furthermore, Gotra-based discrimination also perpetuates the caste system and reinforces the social hierarchy based on Gotras, where people from higher Gotras are considered to be of a higher social status and have more power and privilege. This can lead to discrimination against individuals from lower Gotras in areas such as education, employment, and political representation.

Gotra-based discrimination can also take a violent form, with instances of atrocities and violence committed against individuals and communities from lower Gotras.

It's important to note that Gotra-based discrimination is not a problem specific to rural or isolated areas, but it also exists in urban and developed areas of the country.

Gotra-based discrimination is a serious issue in India that can take various forms such as social exclusion, economic discrimination, and exclusivity in society.

"The culture of India is the mother of all cultures, because it is old, because it sustains."

- Jiddu Krishnamurti

XIV

Gotra Preservation and Revival: A Contemporary Perspective

The Gotra system, which traces lineage from a common male ancestor, is an important aspect of social identity in many parts of India. While the traditional practice of Gotra exogamy has been used to preserve certain Gotras, the changing times and modern perspectives have led to a renewed interest in preserving and reviving Gotras. This chapter aims to explore this contemporary perspective on Gotra preservation and revival.

One of the main reasons for the renewed interest in Gotra preservation is the recognition of the cultural and historical significance of Gotras. Many individuals and communities have begun to see the value in preserving and passing down their Gotra lineage as an important aspect of their cultural heritage.

Another reason for the renewed interest in Gotra preservation is the recognition of the importance of inclusivity and equality in society. Many individuals and communities have begun to challenge the traditional practice of Gotra exogamy and have started to marry within their Gotra, leading to the preservation of Gotras that were previously at risk of disappearing.

The renewed interest in Gotra preservation has also led to an increase in the study and documentation of Gotras, including genealogical research and the creation of Gotra databases.

The Gotra system is an important aspect of social identity in many parts of India. While the traditional practice of Gotra exogamy has been used to preserve certain Gotras, a contemporary perspective recognizes the cultural and historical significance of Gotras and the importance of inclusivity and equality in society. This has led to a renewed interest in preserving and reviving Gotras, through the practice of Gotra endogamy, genealogical research, and the creation of Gotra databases. This renewed interest in Gotra preservation not only helps in preserving the cultural heritage but also helps in creating a more inclusive society, where people are not discriminated based on their Gotra. It's important for individuals and communities to strike a balance between preserving their Gotra heritage and promoting inclusivity and equality in society.

"The spiritual heritage of India is the most precious treasure that mankind possesses."

- Swami Vivekananda

୫

XV

The Future of Gotras in India

The Gotra system, which traces lineage from a common male ancestor, is an important aspect of social identity in many parts of India. Throughout this book, we have explored the origins, significance, and impact of the Gotra system on Indian society and culture.

The future of Gotras in India is uncertain, as it depends on various factors such as social, economic, and political developments. However, it's important to note that the Gotra system has undergone changes over time and will continue to evolve in the future.

One possible future for Gotras in India is that they may become increasingly irrelevant in the face of modernity and globalization, as people become more focused on education, career, and personal growth, rather than lineage and tradition. This can lead to a decline in the importance of Gotras and the practice of Gotra exogamy.

On the other hand, there is a possibility that Gotras may continue to be an important aspect of social identity in India, especially in rural and traditional communities. In this scenario, efforts to preserve and revive Gotras may become increasingly important.

In any case, it's important to recognize that the Gotra system is not a monolithic entity and that its significance and practice may vary among different regions and communities. It's also important to acknowledge that the Gotra system, like any other tradition, can be a source of discrimination and exclusivity and it's important to strive for inclusivity and equality in society.

The future of Gotras in India is uncertain and depends on various factors. However, it's important to recognize that the Gotra system is not a monolithic entity and that its significance and practice may vary among different regions and communities. It's also important to acknowledge that the Gotra system, like any other tradition, can be a source of discrimination and exclusivity and it's important to strive for inclusivity and equality in society.

"India is the one country in the world where spiritualism and science are not in conflict."

- Dr. APJ Abdul Kalam

XVI

Name Titles names per Gotra prevalent in India

It's worth noting that these are some of the most common and well-known Gotra names in India but not exhaustive, and there are many more Gotra names depending on different regions and communities. Also, it's important to note that one's gotra is not only limited to their surname but also inherited from their father's lineage.

Bhardwaj

Kashyap

Sharma

Kaushik

Tiwari

Gautam

Jain

Vashisht

Agarwal
Gupta
Khatri
Mittal
Rajput
Chauhan
Parmar
Patel
Mehta
Seth
Bhatnagar
Shukla
Trivedi
Pandey
Dave
Desai
Modi
Shah
Kothari
Mehta
Deshpande
Joshi
Jha
Chaudhary
Nair
Menon
Iyer
Bose
Banerjee
Reddy
Naidu
Srivastava
Patil

Rao
Chakraborty
Mukherjee
Das
Mallick
Sen
Lahiri
Gandhi
Birla
Kaul
Dixit
Saini
Bhanushali
Dutta
Kachhwaha
Chaudhary
Kshatriya
Bhatia
Rana
Upadhyay
Sengar
Rawat
Bisht
Khandelwal
Tandon
Bhandari
Meena
Solanki
Gahlot
Raghuvanshi
Thakur
Kshatriya
Khatri

Bishnoi
Nambissan
Jangid
Jangra
Kanyakubj
Jadaun
Kachwaha
Lodha
Kahar
Khatik
Kori

OTHER BOOKS OF THE AUTHOR

1. The Moments When I Met God
2. Kashiyile Theertha Pathangal
3. GURU GYAN VANI
4. Abhiprerak Gita
5. ASSI SE JAIN GHAT TAK
6. Hopelessness of Arjuna
7. The Soul and It's True Nature
8. Sense of Action (Karma)
9. Action through Wisdom
10. Action through Wisdom
11. THEORY AND PRACTICAL OF EVERY ACTION
12. LOGICAL UNDERSTANDING OF THE SUPREME
13. THE IMPERISHABLE SUPREME
14. Yatra Nishadraj se Hanuman Ghat Tak
15. Yatra Karnatak Ghat se Raja Ghat Tak
16. Yatra Pandey Ghat se Prayagraj Ghat Tak
17. Yatra Ranjendra Prasad Ghat se Dattatreya Ghat Tak
18. YaatraSindhiya Ghat se Gwaliar Ghat Tak
19. Yatra Mangala Gauri Ghat se Hanuman Gadhi Ghat Tak
20. Yatra Gaay Ghat Se Nishad Ghat Tak
21. MAA GANGA, GHATEN EVM UTSAV
22. Ganga Arti Dev Deepavali evam Any Utsav
23. Potentials of Digitalized India
24. VEDIC CONSCIOUSNESS
25. A Brief Introduction to Vedic Science
26. Kashi ke Barah Jyotirling
27. IMPACT OF MOTIVATION
28. Let's have a Milky Way Journey
29. Color Therapy in a Nutshell

59. The Holistic Cow: A Look at the Physical, Spiritual, and Cultural Importance of Cows in India
60. Arts of Healing
61. Exploring the Divine
62. Understanding Five Elements
63. The Etymology of Ram
64. Symbols of India
65. Voice of Change (About Speeches of Great Men)
66. She Speaks (About Speeches of Great Women)
67. Patriotism on Celluloid – Brief About Patriotic Films
68. The Music of Motivation: A Brief Guide to Inspirational Film Songs
69. **Unlocking the Secrets of the Dashopanishads**
70. A Cultural Mosaic
71. Ancient Traditions, Modern Minds
72. Ecos of Ancient Wisdom
73. Beneath the Surface
74. From Temples to Ashrams
75. Sages of the Subcontinent
76. The Art of Healling (Ayurveda, Yoga & Naturopathy)
77. Indian Kitchen
78. The Festivals of India
79. The Indian Epics Retold
80. The Power of Mantras
81. The Indian River Ganges
82. The Indian Architecture
83. Rites of Passage
84. The Indian Silk Road
85. The Indian Literature
86. The Indian Villages
87. The Indian Folks & Crafts
88. The Way of Buddha
89. The Ramayan of Tulsidas

CONTACT

DR. JAGADEESH PILLAI

PhD in Vedic Science

Four Times Guinness World Record Holder

Winner of Mahatma Gandhi Vishwa Shanti Puraskar and
Global Peace Ambassador

Gemology, Astro & Vastu Consultant - Spiritual Counselor

Consultant for designing World Record Ideas

Efficient Tarot Card Reader

9839093003

myrichindia@gmail.com

drjagadeeshpillai@facebook

drjagadeeshpillai@instagram

jagadeeshpillai@youtube

www. JAGADEESHPILLAI.com

৪৩

|| LOKAHA SAMASTHAHA SUKHINO BHAVANTU ||